Best
West Virginia
Recipes

Diana Loera

Other Books by Diana Loera

12 Extra Special Summer Dessert Fondue Recipes http://tinyurl.com/q7gpgw8

Fast Start Guide to Flea Market Selling http://tinyurl.com/qb83smw

14 Extra Special Winter Holidays Fondue Recipes http://tinyurl.com/lkebggx

Awesome Thanksgiving Leftovers Revive Guide http://tinyurl.com/prxjayg

Stop Hot Flashes Now http://tinyurl.com/kxmr8ps

Party Time Chicken Wing Recipes http://tinyurl.com/ohsc9x8

Summertime Sangria http://tinyurl.com/oxnlnhm

Please visit www.LoeraPublishingLLC.com to see our complete selection of books.

Topics include cooking, travel, recipes, how to, non- fiction and more.

Table of Contents

Introduction

I was introduced to West Virginia home cooking as a child.

The mother of one of my father's horse trainers hailed from the mighty coal mining state – West Virginia.

 I can still smell those pepperoni rolls cooking when we walked into this wonderful lady's home.

A true lady and a gifted cook, she deftly crafted countless down home recipes.

Of course, I never thought to write down those recipes and have thought about green tomato pie and other recipes over the years with fond memories.

 Memories of that time long ago came flooding back once again when recently talking with someone from West Virginia.

I compiled a selection of West Virginia recipes from recipes that I remembered from my childhood and also recipes that I had recently discussed with a West Virginian aka Mountaineer.

I know these are only the tip of the iceberg when it comes to West Virginia but I hope that you find at least one recipe that brings back memories if you hail from West Virginia or introduces you to a new favorite.

I've also included a few photographs from the turn of the century featuring West Virginia residents. I love old photos and if you do too, I hope you like the ones I've included.

So, enough talking – let's move on so you can see these recipes and photographs.

One last comment before we do so – I would like to thank Kim for inspiring me to create this book. She is originally from West Virginia and my conversations with her about her beloved West Virginia is what made the idea of this book come to life.

Cool Photos Taken in West Virginia in the early 1900's

Following are just a few cool photos that I came across recently. They are from the early 1900's and feature West Virginia residents.

Those years were definitely a different lifestyle and different mindset.

 I selected a few photos that I thought captured the spirit, grit and determination of West Virginia residents.

Cool Photos Taken in West Virginia in the early 1900's

Title: Richwood, West Virginia. (vicinity) Hazel Friend cooking lunch in her little mountain home

Creator(s): Collier, John, 1913-1992, photographer

Date Created/Published: 1942 Sept.

Title: A "Demonstration team" composed of three prize-winning Cabell County girls. They are showing the visitors at the Fair how team work makes for efficiency in canning their farm products. State 4 H. Fair, Charleston, W. Va. Location: Charleston, West Virginia / Photo by Lewis W. Hine.

Creator(s): Hine, Lewis Wickes, 1874-1940, photographer

Date Created/Published: 1921 October 13.

Title: Coal miners waiting for the bus, eating ice cream suckers (popsicles). Pursglove, West Virginia

Creator(s): Wolcott, Marion Post, 1910-1990, photographer

Date Created/Published: 1938 Sept.

Title: Lunch Time, Economy Glass Works, Morgantown, W. Va. Plenty more like this, inside. Location: Morgantown, West Virginia.

Creator(s): Hine, Lewis Wickes, 1874-1940, photographer

Title: Mother, wife and child of unemployed coal miner, Marine, West Virginia

Creator(s): Wolcott, Marion Post, 1910-1990, photographer

Date Created/Published: 1938 Sept.

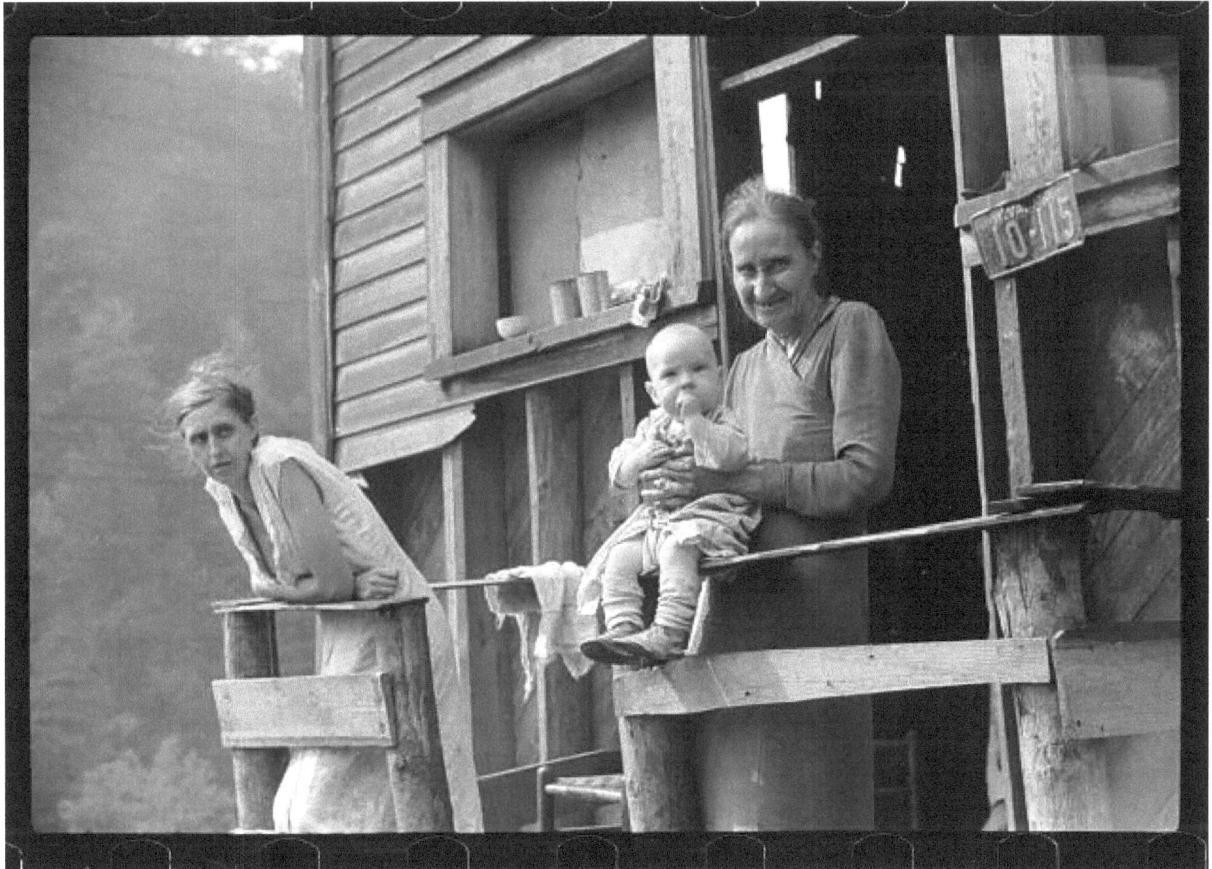

Title: Bank boss, (with lamp between knees) Motorman, Brake-boy and Driver. Gary Mine, Gary, W. Va. Boss said he would use more boys if he could get them but they went to school. Note live wire on level with heads. Location: Gary, West Virginia.

Creator(s): Hine, Lewis Wickes, 1874-1940, photographer

Date Created/Published: 1908 September.

Title: Farm women come to town on Saturday afternoon to sell eggs, milk, cakes, etc., in the courthouse square. Morgantown, West Virginia

Creator(s): Wolcott, Marion Post, 1910-1990, photographer

Date Created/Published: 1938 Sept.

West Virginia Pie

1 stick butter, melted & cooled

1 c. sugar

1/2 c. flour

2 eggs, slightly beaten

1 tsp. vanilla

1 c. pecans, broken

16 oz. pkg. chocolate chips

Directions

Mix sugar and flour.

Add eggs, butter, pecans, chocolate chips (unmelted), vanilla.

Pour into pie shell (unbaked).

Bake at 325 degrees for 1 hour.

Serve slightly warm with whipped cream.

West Virginia Pie

Brunswick Stew

Starting with the sauce -

In a 2 quart sauce pan, over low heat-

Melt ¼ cup of butter then add:

1¾ cups Ketchup

¼ cup French's Yellow Mustard

¼ cup white vinegar

Blend until smooth

Then add-

½ tablespoon chopped garlic

1 teaspoon coarse ground black pepper

½ teaspoon crushed red pepper

½ oz. Liquid Smoke

1 oz. Worcestershire Sauce

1 oz. Hot Sauce or ½ oz. Tabasco

½ tablespoon fresh lemon juice

Blend until smooth, then add:

¼ cup dark brown sugar

Stir constantly, increase heat to simmer (DO NOT BOIL) for approx. 10 minutes.

Makes approx. 3½ cups of sauce (set aside - to be added later).

Part 2- the Stew:

In a 2 gallon pot, over low heat melt ¼ lb. of butter then add-

3 cups small diced potatoes

1 cup small diced onion

2 14½ oz. cans of chicken broth

1 lb. baked chicken shredded off bone (white and dark)

8-10 oz. smoked pork

Bring to a rolling boil, stirring until potatoes are near done, then add-

1 8½ oz. can small June early peas

2   14½ oz. cans stewed tomatoes - (chop tomatoes, add liquid to the stew pot)

The sauce made above

1 16 oz. can of baby lima beans

¼ cup Liquid Smoke

1 14½ oz. can creamed corn

Slow simmer for 2 hours

Apple Butter Drop Cookies

Makes about 2 dozen cookies

Ingredients:

1/4 cup sugar

1/2 cup shortening

1 cup apple butter

1 teaspoon baking soda

2-1/4 cup flour

1/2 teaspoon salt

1 teaspoon baking powder

1/2 cup milk

1/2 teaspoon vanilla

1/2 cup nuts

Directions:

Preheat oven to 350° F. and grease cookie sheet.

In a bowl, cream sugar and shortening.

Add apple butter and baking soda.

Add flour, salt and baking powder alternately with milk. Mix well.

Add vanilla and nuts.

Drop by teaspoon onto prepared cookie sheet.

Bake for 10 to 12 minutes.

Remove from oven and let cool.

West Virginia Old Fashioned Blackberry Cake

1 1/2 c. sugar

1/2 c. butter or Crisco

2 c. flour

1/2 c. buttermilk

2 tsp. nutmeg

2 c. blackberries

5 eggs

2 tsp. baking soda

2 tsp. cinnamon

1/2 c. cloves

Cream sugar, shortening, and eggs.

Mix together flour, baking soda, cinnamon, nutmeg, and clove.

Add to shortening mix, then mix in buttermilk.

Add blackberries last.

Bake in greased and floured tube pan at 350 degrees for 1 hour.

Remove from oven and allow to cool.

Frost with caramel or vanilla icing.

West Virginia Coal Miner Milk Gravy

This is true make from scratch recipe. You'll want to serve it over homemade biscuits. There are no measurements as you'll read below. I think it would ruin the heritage and charm of this recipe to put in actual measurements. A cast iron skillet works best.

Bacon Grease

Water

Evaporated Milk

Flour

Salt

Pepper

Directions

Leave a good amount of bacon grease in the skillet after you've cooked bacon, along with any brown cracklings from the bacon itself.

Let the skillet stay hot as you sprinkle in the flour.

Brown the flour until the skillet almost smokes. When you almost think you have burned the flour, keep stirring it in with the grease.

It shouldn't be too thin or too thick. Only practice will tell you how much flour to put in.

Then add water, cutting down the heat slightly.

Stir vigorously, mixing the water into the browned flour and grease, until it is quite thin.

It will take a lot more water than you think.

When you have a pretty good amount of the mixture, add in evaporated milk; stir it in well; add a bit of salt and a lot of pepper; then let it simmer until it gets back to the thickness you want. This should only take one to two minutes.

Pour the gravy over hot biscuits. Serve and enjoy.

West Virginia Reese's Cups Cookie Bars

2 sticks margarine or butter, room temperature

1 cup peanut butter – creamy preferred

1 lb. confectioners' sugar

1 1/2 cups graham cracker crumbs

16-oz milk chocolate chips

In a large bowl, cream together the margarine, peanut butter, confectioners' sugar, graham cracker crumbs. Mix together thoroughly and pat into the bottom of a 9 x 13-inch dish or pan.

Melt the chocolate chips in the microwave or over hot water, stirring until totally melted. Spread the chocolate over the peanut butter layer.

Let chocolate set before cutting into bars.

Huckleberry Pie

Ingredients:

1 recipe pastry for a 9 inch double crust pie or buy an unbaked pie shell

4 cups huckleberries

2 1/2 tablespoons tapioca

2/3 cup white sugar

1/4 teaspoon salt

1/2 cup packed brown sugar

1 tablespoon cider vinegar

1 tablespoon butter

Directions:

1. Mix together the huckleberries, tapioca, sugar, salt, brown sugar, and apple cider vinegar.

2. Pour mixture into unbaked pie shell. Dot top with butter. Add top pastry and flute edges.

3. Bake at 400 degrees F (205 degrees C) for 15 minutes. Then turn oven down to 350 degrees F (175 degrees C) for 45-55 minutes.

Huckleberry Pie

Green Tomato Pie

1 recipe pastry for a 9 inch double crust pie

4 cups sliced green tomatoes

1 1/4 cups white sugar

1 teaspoon lemon juice

2 tablespoons all-purpose flour

1 teaspoon ground cinnamon

1 pinch ground nutmeg

1 pinch salt

2 tablespoons butter

DIRECTIONS

Preheat oven to 375 degrees F. Roll pastry and line a 9 inch deep-dish pie plate.

In a large bowl, combine sliced tomatoes, sugar, lemon juice, flour, cinnamon, nutmeg and salt. Toss lightly to mix. Pour into pastry lined deep-dish pie plate.

Put little dabs of butter in about 4 or 5 places around the top of pie then cover with pastry. Make slits wherever you please.

Bake at 375 degrees F (190 degrees C) for 10 minutes then reduce heat to 350 degrees F (175 degrees C) and continue baking until golden and bubbly.

Green Tomato Pie

Grandma's West Virginia Mayonnaise Cake

2 cups flour

2 tsp. baking soda

3 level tbsp. baking cocoa

Mix the above three ingredients together.

Using a second bowl mix together the following -

1 cup sugar

1 cup mayonnaise

1 cup cold water

1 tsp. vanilla

Mix these ingredients and then add in ingredients from the first bowl and mix all together until smooth.

Mix it up a little and then beat in dry ingredients until smooth.

Preheat oven to 350.

Pour above batter into a greased cake pan and bake at 350 degrees for 30-35 minutes.

Put into a greased cake pan and bake at 350 for 30 to 35 minutes.

Remove cake from oven, cool and frost with your favorite frosting.

Cabbage, Sausage, and Apple Soup

2 - 3 tablespoon butter or margarine

3 cups prepared coleslaw mix (available in produce section)

1 med. onion, chopped

1/2 teaspoon thyme

5 cups water

5 chicken bouillon cubes

l/2 lb. smoked sausage, cut up

2 med. unpeeled apples, cored and chopped (about 2 cups)

l/4 teaspoon black pepper

Instructions

Melt margarine or butter in Dutch oven or large saucepan over medium heat.

Add coleslaw mix, onion, and thyme. Cook 5 to 8 minutes until vegetables are crisp tender.

Cover with lid for a few minutes and stir occasionally.

Stir in remaining ingredients and cook partially covered another l5 or 20 minutes until apples are tender and flavors are blended, stir occasionally.

West Virginia Style Barbeque Pulled Pork Sandwiches

Makes 4 hearty sandwiches, be sure to have coleslaw and baked beans on the side. Some people like to put the coleslaw right on the sandwich.

3-1/4 pounds Boston butt roast

2-1/4 cloves garlic, minced

1 teaspoon seasoning salt

1 teaspoon ground black pepper

1/4 teaspoon cayenne pepper

1/2 onion, chopped

1-1/2 cups and 2 tablespoons your favorite barbecue sauce

Rub garlic, seasoning salt, pepper and cayenne pepper to taste onto roast.

Place roast in a large Dutch oven and fill half way with water; add onion.

 Bring to a rolling boil over high heat.

Reduce heat simmer and let cook until meat falls off the bone. This should take at least 3 to 4 hours depending on the size of the roast.

 Place hot roast in a serving bowl and pour on your favorite barbecue sauce. Stir until well blended. Serve on your favorite buns.

West Virginia Style Barbeque Pulled Pork Sandwich

West Virginia Pepperoni Rolls

This book would not be complete without a recipe for Pepperoni Rolls as they are a famous West Virginia specialty.

Ingredients:

1 cup warm water (100 degrees F/40 degrees C)

1/2 teaspoon white sugar

1 (.25 ounce) package active dry yeast

5 cups all-purpose flour

3/4 cup white sugar

2 teaspoons salt

2 eggs, beaten

1/2 cup butter, melted

1 (8 ounce) package sliced pepperoni

Directions:

1. Dissolve 1/2 teaspoon sugar in 1 cup of warm water in a small bowl. Sprinkle yeast over the water and let stand for 5 minutes.

2. Mix flour, 3/4 cup sugar, and salt in a large bowl. Stir in the yeast mixture, beaten eggs, and melted butter. When the dough has pulled together, turn it out onto a lightly floured surface and knead until smooth and elastic, about 8 minutes.

3. Lightly oil a large bowl, then place the dough in the bowl and turn to coat with oil. Cover with a light cloth and let rise in a warm place (80 to 95 degrees F (27 to 35 degrees C)) until doubled in volume, about 1 1/2 hours.

4. Preheat an oven to 350 degrees F (175 degrees C). Grease a cookie sheet.

5. Punch down the dough, and divide it into 20 equal pieces about the size of a golf ball. Using your hands, flatten each piece into a small rectangle about 4 inches square. Place 3 slices of pepperoni down the center of each dough square, overlapping the slices. Place another row of 3 slices next to the first. Roll the dough around the pepperoni slices, pinch the edges closed, and place the rolls on the prepared cookie sheet.

6. Bake the rolls in the preheated oven for 14 to 16 minutes, until the bottoms are lightly browned and the tops are barely golden. Remove from oven and serve warm.

Williamson Firehouse Chili

This famous recipe chili was created by the firefighters at the Williamson, WV fire department. This is by far the most unusual and also the tastiest chili recipe that I've come across thus far.

Ingredients

2 pounds ground beef

2 pounds ground pork

1 tablespoon olive oil

1 large Vidalia onion, diced

4 cloves fresh garlic, chopped

1 (28-ounce) canned whole tomatoes, broken

4 fresh red hot peppers, chopped

1 (12-ounce) tomato paste

6 tablespoons chili powder

1 tablespoon oregano

2 tablespoons cocoa powder

3 teaspoons cumin

1 teaspoon sugar

2 (15½-ounce) cans light red kidney beans

2 (15½-ounce) cans dark red kidney beans

Kosher salt, to taste

Chipotle sauce, to taste

Directions

Mix beef and pork.

Brown meats and drain fat.

Sauté onion and garlic in olive oil.

Combine beef and pork with sautéed onions and garlic.

Add juices from tomatoes and stir.

Add tomatoes, peppers, tomato paste, and spices.

Simmer 2 hours; add beans after 1 hour.

Use bottled water to obtain the consistency desired.

West Virginia Summer Berry Pie

Ingredients

1 unbaked double pie crust, recipe to follow

⅔ to 1 cup sugar

4 tablespoons flour

Dash of salt

3 cups fresh berries

2 tablespoons butter, cut into pieces

1 egg white, lightly beaten

Directions

In a small bowl, mix sugar, flour, and salt

Line 9-inch pie pan with crust

Top fresh berries in crust

Sprinkle sugar mixture over fresh berries

Dot berries with butter pieces and cover with crust

Cut vent openings on top crust

Brush crust with beaten egg white, and sprinkle with white sugar

Bake at 400° for 40 to 50 minutes

Remove from oven and let cool

Serve warm

Even better with a scoop of ice cream or a dollop of whipped cream

West Virginia Baked Beans

West Virginia Baked Beans

2 cups yellow eyed beans

1 yellow onion, chopped

1/2 lb. local bacon, chopped

6 Tablespoons sorghum

1 tsp dry mustard

1 tsp salt

1/4 tsp pepper (or to taste)

Directions

1.Soak beans for 1-2 hours. Drain and simmer in water for 20 minutes. Drain again.

2.Place 1/3 of beans in a Dutch oven. Add 1/3 of onions and 1/3 of bacon. Repeat until everything is used up.

3.Mix remainder of ingredients with at least 1 cup hot water and cover oven.

4.Bake in a 300 degree oven for 4 hours. Occasionally check water levels so beans don't dry out. Stir once or twice during the 4 hours.

West Virginia Summer Berry Compote

Ingredients

2 tablespoons butter

4 cups berries, cleaned and trimmed

½ cup sugar

1 lemon zested and juiced

Pinch of salt

Directions

In a large saucepan, melt the butter over medium-high heat. Add the berries, sugar, lemon zest, and lemon juice.

Cook mixture, stirring often, until the berries begin to break down and release their juices, around 5 minutes.

Remove the pan from the heat and serve on top of French toast.

Carmelized Honey Apples

Ingredients

1 cup brown sugar

1/2 cup unsalted butter

1/2 cup honey

1/4 cup heavy cream

1/4 teaspoon cinnamon, ground

6 apples, washed, dried, with stems removed

6 Popsicle sticks

1/3 cup almonds, sliced (optional)

Directions

Combine brown sugar, butter, honey, cream, and cinnamon in a 2-quart heavy-bottomed saucepan.

Cook over medium-high, stirring constantly, until a candy thermometer reads 265°.

Remove from heat and allow to cool for five minutes. Insert Popsicle stick into the top of each apple through to the center.

Holding apple by the stick, carefully dip in hot honey caramel to coat.

Roll bottom of apple in nuts if desired.

Place on waxed paper to cool.

Repeat with remaining apples.

Bleu Cheese Devilled Eggs

Ingredients

2 tablespoons olive oil

3 slices prosciutto, chopped

1/2 teaspoon garlic, minced

6 large eggs, hard-cooked

1/4 cup mayonnaise

2 tablespoons low-fat bleu cheese, crumbled

1/2 teaspoon Dijon mustard

1/8 teaspoon white pepper, ground

Directions

In small skillet, heat oil over medium heat.

Add prosciutto and garlic; cook for 5 minutes, stirring constantly.

Remove from heat.

Halve eggs lengthwise.

Remove yolks and mash.

Add remaining ingredients and prosciutto mixture until well blended.

Spoon mixture into egg whites.

Chill until ready to serve.

West Virginia Casserole

While this is nothing fancy, it is a good solid warm you up meal. It is fast to prepare and you can use leftover turkey or chicken.

Ingredients:

2 regular size boxes Stove Top stuffing mix, divided. I prefer the Cornbread flavor but you can use Chicken or Turkey favors too.

2 cups bite-size pieces cooked chicken or turkey

1 can cream of chicken soup

1 can cream of mushroom soup

Directions:

Preheat oven to 350°F.

Follow the direction on the box to prepare 2 boxes of stuffing mix. I usually use the microwave method on the box

Place one half stuffing in a greased casserole dish and set the other half aside

Add chicken or turkey

In a bowl, mix together the 2 cans of soup

Pour the soup over the casserole mixture and pour over the mixture.

Top the mixture with the remaining stuffing

Bake for 30-35 minutes

I prefer to bake for about ten minutes, then lightly cover with tin foil – leaving the ends of the dish open.

Uncover totally the last 5 to 7 minutes of baking.

You can decide if my tin foil method or a variation of it works for you. The original recipe states to bake uncovered the entire time. In my case I felt it was too dry when done.

Remove from oven, allow to slightly cool and then serve.

West Virginia Stew

1 lb. beef, cut into 1" cubes

2 1/2 c. boiling water

1 chopped onion

1/2 tsp. salt

1/2 tsp. Worcestershire sauce

1/4 tsp. pepper

1/4 tsp. paprika

Dash of allspice

1 tsp. sugar

1/4 c. tomato juice

1 c. sliced carrots

1 c. cubed potatoes

1 c. diced celery

Brown meat in hot fat.

Add hot water, onion, lemon juice, seasonings and tomato juice.

Simmer for 2 hours.

 Add more water if needed.

Add vegetables and cook until done.

Cheddar Bacon Butter

Ingredients

1/2 cup softened butter

1/2 cup shredded cheddar cheese

1/4 cup crumbled bacon bits

2 tablespoons chopped fresh chives

Directions

In a small bowl, combine all ingredients. Mix well.

Great on corn on the cob, oven toasted bread, corn bread, grilled steak and more

West Virginia Skillet Casserole

1 pounds Ground beef

1 cup Chopped green pepper

1 cup Chopped onion

1 can Tomato sauce; (15 oz.)

1½ teaspoon Chili powder

½ teaspoon Salt

½ teaspoon Pepper

1 cup Flour

¾ cup Cornmeal

¼ cup Sugar

1 tablespoon Baking powder

½ teaspoon Salt

1 Egg,beaten

1 cup Milk

¼ cup Vegetable oil

Preheat oven to 400 F

In 10-inch cast iron skillet, brown ground beef, green peppers, and onions, and then drain the grease.

Add tomato sauce, chili powder, salt and pepper; simmer 15 minutes.

 Meanwhile, mix together dry ingredients.

Combine egg, milk and oil; stir into dry ingredients just until moistened.

Pour batter over beef mixture and bake in preheated 400F oven about 30 minutes or until golden and cornbread is done in the center.

Remove from oven and serve.

Makes 4 generous portions.

West Virginia Cornbread

1 c. cornmeal

1 c. whole flour

1/4 c. oil

1 sm. onion, chopped

1-2 c. milk

1/4 c. sugar

1/2 c. grated sharp cheese

1/2 c. creamed corn

1/4 tsp. salt

2 tsp. baking powder

Options

1/8 tsp. red pepper flakes or a jalapeno pepper, chopped

Mix the above and stir well. The batter will be somewhat lumpy.

Preheat oven to 350F

In an iron skillet, heat 2 tablespoons Crisco.

Melt shortening until almost smoking.

Pour batter into skillet.

Bake 30-35 minutes at 375 degrees.

Carefully remove from oven, slice and serve warm

West Virginia Skillet Cornbread

West Virginia Molasses Ginger Cookies

1/3 c. molasses

1 c. shortening (butter flavor Crisco)

1 c. sugar (plus some for rolling)

1 egg

2 c. flour

2 tsp. baking soda

1/2 tsp. ginger

1 tsp. cinnamon

1/2 tsp. cloves, ground

Preheat oven to 350 degrees.

In large bowl cream sugar, shortening; add molasses, egg, mix until well blended.

In small bowl sift together dry ingredients.

Add gradually to shortening mixture until well blended.

Chill mixture at least 1 hour.

When well chilled, with hands make 1 inch balls of dough and roll in sugar.

Bake immediately on ungreased cookie sheet 10-12 minutes or until centers look dry but not firm.

Cookies should be flexible, not crisp.

Remove from oven, cool and place in an airtight container.

West Virginia Molasses Ginger Cookies

Thank you for taking the time to read my book.

I'm always interested in trying new recipes, if you have a West Virginia recipe that is just too good to not share- you're more than welcome to email me at

LoeraPublishing@hotmail.com

Sincerely,

Diana

www.ingramcontent.com/pod-product-compliance
Lightning Source LLC
Chambersburg PA
CBHW042059040426
42448CB00002B/72